W9-BNF-966

MYTHOLOGY and
LEGENDS around
the WORLD

Norse Myths and Legends

Edited by Joanne Randolph

Cavendish
Square

New York

Published in 2018 by Cavendish Square Publishing, LLC
243 5th Avenue, Suite 136, New York, NY 10016

Cataloging-in-Publication Data

Names: Randolph, Joanne, editor.
Title: Norse myths and legends / edited by Joanne Randolph.
Description: New York : Cavendish Square Publishing, 2018. | Series: Mythology and legends around the world | Includes bibliographical references and index.
Identifiers: ISBN 9781502632784 (library bound) | ISBN 9781502634634 (pbk.) | ISBN 9781502633095 (ebook)
Subjects: LCSH: Mythology, Norse--Juvenile literature.
Classification: LCC BL860.R36 2018 | DDC 293/.13--dc23

Editorial Director: David McNamara
Editor: Caitlyn Miller
Copy Editor: Rebecca Rohan
Associate Art Director: Amy Greenan
Designer: Megan Metté
Production Coordinator: Karol Szymczuk
Photo Research: J8 Media

"Who Were the Norse People?" by Barbara Krasner-Khait from *Calliope* Magazine (January 2003)
"The Eddas: Iceland's Book of Lore" by Kimberly Zarins from *Calliope* Magazine (January 2003)
"Yggdrasil, The Sacred Ash Tree" by Gloria W. Lannom from *Calliope* Magazine (January 2003)
"Welcome to Valhalla!" by Deborah Nourse Lattimore from *Calliope* Magazine (January 2003)
"Balder's Dream" by Deborah Nourse Lattimore from *Calliope* Magazine (January 2003)
"Ragnarok" by Deborah Nourse Lattimore from *Calliope* Magazine (January 2003)
"Thor's Wedding" from *Appleseeds* Magazine (February 2012)

All articles © by Carus Publishing Company. Reproduced with permission.

All Cricket Media material is copyrighted by Carus Publishing Company, d/b/a Cricket Media, and/or various authors and illustrators. Any commercial use or distribution of material without permission is strictly prohibited. Please visit http://www.cricketmedia.com/info/licensing2 for licensing and http://www.cricketmedia.com for subscriptions.

The photographs in this book are used by permission and through the courtesy of: Cover, AF Fotografie/Alamy Stock; p. 4 Fine Art Images/Heritage Images/Getty Images; p. 7 DEA/M. Seemuller/De Agostini/Getty Images; p. 8 Softeis, own work/File: Gokstad-ship-model.jpg/Wikimedia Commons; p. 9 Prisma/UIG/Getty Images; pp. 10-11, 15, Photo © O. Vaering/Bridgeman Images; pp. 12-13 Standret/Shutterstock.com; p. 16 Werner Forman Archive/Bridgeman Images; p. 19 Inger Helene Boasson/NordicPhotos/Age fotostock; pp. 20-21 Vuk Kostic/Shutterstock.com; p. 22 Helen Stratton/A book of myths (1915) New York : G. P Putnam's sons; London, T. C. & E. C. Jack. Copy at New York Public Library, scanned by nicole_deyo, obtained from http://www.archive.org/details/bookofmyths00lang/File: Freya, Queen of the Northern Gods, A Book of Myths.jpg/Wikimedia Commons; pp. 24-25 Guttorm Raknes (Drguttorm), own work/File: Brennviksanden.jpg/Wikimedia Commons; p. 26 © Look and Learn/Bridgeman Images; p. 29 Gunnar Creutz, own work/File: Karlevistenen Öl1 (Raä-nr Vickleby 10-1) 0544.jpg/Wikimedia Commons; p. 30 Chronicle/Mary Evans Picture Library/Alamy Stock Photo; p. 31 Arthur Rackham (1867–1939) (illus) (August 1924) [1911] Siegfried & The Twilight of the Gods (http://www.archive.org/details/siegfriedtwiligh00wagn) (New Impression ed.), London: William Heinemann, p. 108 Retrieved on 22 June 2011/File: Siegfried and the Twilight of the Gods p 108.jpg/Wikimedia Commons; p. 33 Emil Doepler (1855–1922) ca. 1905, Walhall, die Götterwelt der Germanen. Martin Oldenbourg, Berlin. Photographed by Haukurth (talk contribs) and cropped by Bloodofox (talk contribs)/File: Walhall by Emil Doepler.jpg /Wikimedia Commons; p. 35 W. T. Maud, 1890/File: Valkyries by W. T. Maud.jpg/Wikimedia Commons; p. 36 Werner Forman/UIG/Getty Images; p. 43 Bettmann/Getty Images; p. 44 John Charles Dollman (1851–1934)/Guerber, H. A. (Hélène Adeline) (1909). Myths of the Norsemen from the Eddas and Sagas. London: Harrap, illustration facing page 210. Digitized by the Internet Archive and available from http://www.archive.org/details/mythsofthenorsem00gueruoft Some simple image processing by User: Haukurth/File: Hermod before Hela.jpg/Wikimedia Commons; pp. 48-49 Louis Moe (1857–1945)/Danmarks Historie i Billeder, 1898, København, Danmark/ Fra Dansk Skolemuseum/File: Balders Bålfærd (17005-1).jpg/Wikimedia Commons; p. 50 Hamilton Wright Mabie,1908. Norse Stories Retold from the Eddas. Dodd, Mead and Company, New York. Page 240. Digitized version from the Internet Archive/File: Then the awful fight began by George Wright (1872-1951).jpg/ Wikimedia Commons; pp. 52-53 Emil Doepler (1855-1922) ca. 1905. Walhall, die Götterwelt der Germanen. Martin Oldenbourg, Berlin. File: Odin und Fenriswolf Freyr und Surt.jpg/Wikimedia Commons; p. 54 MaryquiZe/Shutterstock.com; p. 56 3gGd_ynWqGjGfQ at Google Cultural Institute (https://www.google.com/culturalinstitute/asset-viewer/3gGd_ynWqGjGfQ) maximum zoom level/File: Mårten Eskil Winge (1825-1896) - Tor's Fight with the Giants - Google Art Project.jpg/Wikimedia Commons; pp. 58-59 The Elder or Poetic Edda; commonly known as Sæmund's Edda. Edited and translated with introduction and notes by Olive Bray, Illustrated by W.G. Collingwood (1854 - 1932) ca. 1908, Page 127. Digitized by the Internet Archive and available from http://www.archive.org/details/elderorpoeticedd01brayuoft Image was made from the JPEG 2000 image of the relevant page via image processing (crop, rotate, color-levels, mode) with the GIMP by User: Haukurth version public domain/File: Thrym's Wedding-feast.jpg/Wikimedia Commons.

Printed in the United States of America

Contents

Who Were the Norse People?

The Norse people trace their ancestry to a number of Germanic tribes. The Angles and Saxons, for example, called the base of the Jutland peninsula (present-day Denmark) their home. The Suevi lived on the Baltic coast. The Goths lived along the Vistula River in what is today Poland. And the Lombards ("Longbeards") lived along the Elbe River.

Restlessness during the third through sixth centuries led these and other tribes to a period of continual movement known as the Migration of Nations.

They seized the lands left unprotected by the fall of the Roman Empire and its armies in 476 CE. During the same period, the Angles and Saxons moved west into England. The Suevi and Goths moved to the south. The Lombards headed farther south to present-day Italy. Everywhere the tribes went, they brought with them their beliefs and oral

Opposite: A monk named Abbo of Fleury created this image of Viking ships headed to Britain.

traditions. Proud of their heritage, they looked to the gods to watch over them in battle, to bless them with good crops and economic prosperity, and to control the sky, thunder, and rain for their benefit.

The Viking Age

Turmoil erupted in the new settlements as rivalry between tribes led to a struggle to prove which group was the strongest. As the tribes absorbed one another, a great period of expansion called the Viking Age began in the ninth and tenth centuries. The term "Viking" was first coined around 800 CE and was used to describe all Scandinavians. The Viking world was tough; the weather was harsh and the seas were stormy. Using superb maritime skills and ships equipped with newly invented sails, Vikings stormed villages, monasteries, and churches across northern Europe. They sought security from enemies, trade, and adventure.

The first destinations were to the west: Ireland, where they founded the settlement that today is Dublin, the capital of Ireland; Normandy; and the islands of the Shetlands, Orkneys, and Faroes, and the Isle of Man.

Opposite: This 1440 map shows areas of Greenland and North America that the Vikings discovered. It is the oldest map of these regions. It might look unfamiliar; modern map-making techniques have produced much more accurate maps.

The Vikings have long been famous for their shipbuilding and navigational skills.

Beginning in 834, they targeted continental Europe and the lands of the Franks and the Frisians. The Swedes headed east and sailed up Russia's rivers, making a permanent home in Novgorod and later founding a Scandinavian empire in Kiev. Six thousand settlers made new homes in Iceland in the late ninth century. They brought with them their love of poetry. After a copy of Snorri Sturluson's book *Prose **Edda*** was discovered in an old farmhouse in the seventeenth century, its verses soon became a major source of information about the Norse ancestors.

A Far Reach

The Vikings also reached as far as America in the west, Spain in the south, and Constantinople in the east. Their fast sailing ships were key to two major activities: raids and trade. Shrewd traders, they embarked on large-scale ventures to control international trade. The Vikings were the first people to sail around the European continent and the first to set foot on four continents. They both fought and traded with Native American Indians, Eskimos, Finns, Turks, Slavs, Irish, Franks, Spaniards, English, and Germans, as well as among themselves. Viking influence spread far and wide, as the inscriptions they cut on ancient tombs and monuments can attest.

The National Museum of Denmark has this stone with Viking inscriptions in their collection.

Viking ambitions led to a great age not only of commerce but also of Scandinavian art and craftsmanship.

The Fall of the Norse Gods

By the eighth century, most of the Germanic tribes in continental Europe had chosen Christianity over their own ancient gods. The Norse people were the last to adopt Christianity, ending about 1,000 years of worshipping native deities. Only in the tenth and eleventh centuries did Norwegian kings Olaf Tryggvason and Olaf the Holy first wage battle against the old beliefs. This battle forced many to choose between emigrating or facing death.

For a while, Iceland, which had no king to enforce Christian practices, had provided safe haven for those who clung to the Norse gods. However, by the year 1000, even the Icelandic

Nils Bergslien (1853—1928) painted this depiction of King Tryggvason's Battle of Svolder.

The Vikings lived in villages that looked like this one.

Assembly voted in favor of Christianity, followed by the Danes in 1015 and the Swedes by 1164. Because they were the last to adopt the new faith, Norse literature and artifacts provided the greatest amount of information about these gods and myths.

Norse Values

Although often seen as violent and brutal, Norsemen loved a well-told story and appreciated culture, fine art, craftsmanship, and wit. They took pride in their beautiful and practical ships and swords and were intensely loyal to their chieftains (the political leaders of their districts) and to their kings and jarls (noblemen). The Norse people were also fiercely loyal to their kin. In fact, the Norse home or farmstead typically housed a community of some twenty or thirty relatives. They were tied to the land of their fathers, which passed from generation to generation.

In Norse culture, women were well respected and shared responsibilities as equal partners. In Norse culture, if a man was prepared to die for his beliefs, he was honored. Faith in fair play, the power of the individual, the right to freedom, and the Norse gods shaped these people and their achievements.

Men and women enjoyed equal status in Norse society.

...hverfir of ser, en þi heitr þicka m oskylld ær hã nẽr kveþ sẽt
áþ heitr kvirian þyrnir heið þyrnir leptr hrioðr við blaiṇ
ónin sẽ kenir himinin, kalla k ymiṣ hauṣ ʒ erfiði ʒ byrþi
dǫga hvalm austra vestra norðra syðra tǫ solar ʒ ꝩnglṣ
ʒ hiṃtungla við þa erueþra hialm · hꝥ loptz ʒ varþar ·

Þesi ero nǫ[fn] stundana · aulld · ꜵfum
allda · þyri longu · opstærri · vet[r] sumar haust var · mánoð · vika
þar nótt morgin aptãñ · ꝏlld arla · Snẽma siþla · Iṣiṇ eyria dag
nẽt iger · Sꝛ ẽrel · þ̃ eð heiti nætrinar i olviṣ malum
þ̃ heitir nótt · niola helio · kꝯlluð er grima mʒ guþu oldg
katla ꝛottar · Þar sveṇganñan ñvaar druum
unſi nærin mulin mylin ny hꝥ atalt
þengvet blina ſkynðir ſkálgr ſkramr ·

þolſæna rꜵkull eygloa an ſkip ſyin þaꝝ hvel lino ſtan
ſvalmſteiia alfravþull · Hꝑng ſẽ kenir ſol kalla halꝺvꝛ
eꝑundilþera · ſ mana · kenv gleſ ellde hiṃ ꝝ ʒ laſʒ

her lyṣ
ſ[...]ad
ʒon iꝯjꝝ

The *Eddas*: Iceland's Lore

How do we know about the ancient myths of the Norse people? **Rune** stones, carvings, and other archaeological remains from pagan times preserve some information, but the richest sources are two books from medieval Iceland that were compiled in the thirteenth century: the *Poetic Edda* and the *Prose Edda*.

The Icelanders, who converted to Christianity in the year 1000, no longer believed in the Norse gods, but they still cherished the myths as a part of their heritage. Scholars debate the meaning of the word *"edda."* Some think it translates as "poetry"; others, as "great-grandmother." This second definition suggests an *edda* contains stories passed down orally over many generations. The *Poetic Edda* contains poems, each with its own individual title, about different myths and legends. Many of these poems were recited during

Opposite: A fourteenth-century copy of the *Prose Edda*

the period before Christianity and then written down centuries later. It is amazing that the *Poetic Edda* survived the Middle Ages, since the poems were preserved in only one or two manuscripts. While the *Poetic Edda*'s compiler is unknown, we know that Snorri Sturluson wrote the *Prose Edda* in 1220. Snorri was an influential politician and twice held Iceland's highest public office, the Law-Speaker. Despite his busy schedule, he carefully preserved Norse myths and early poems for future generations.

The Prophecy

One of the themes in the *Poetic Edda* is Odin's continuous search for wisdom. Odin is the king of the gods in Norse mythology. His desire for secret knowledge often led Odin to mysterious places such as Mimir's well, which gave wisdom to all who drank from it. Odin sacrificed an eye for just one precious drink, and that is why he is known as the one-eyed god. Odin also visited the **giants**, because some members of this ancient race had special visionary powers. In the poem "Voluspa" (or "The Seeress's Prophecy"), Odin visits an ancient prophetess who lives among the giants and tells him about the world's beginning and end. Her words are

A statue commemorating Snorri Sturluson stands in Reykholt, Iceland.

mysterious, but Snorri's more complete account in his *Prose Edda* helps us understand these myths.

In the beginning, the universe was barren except for a region of deadly heat and another of poisonous ice. Ymir, the first and most massive of all giants, took shape between these regions. After he perspired, more giants took shape under his left arm and between his legs. There was also a cow that licked the ice to form Buri, a godlike figure. Buri's son Bor married a giantess and became Odin's father. The gods, then, were partly descended from the giants. The seeress is vague on how the gods created the world. Snorri tells us the gruesome details: Odin and his brothers killed Ymir and used his body as the raw material for the universe.

Odin is one of the best-known Norse gods. Some people refer to him by the names Wodan, Woden, or Wotan.

Ymir's blood became the sea; his skull, the sky; his bones, the rocks; and his flesh, the earth. Despite this violent beginning, the world became beautiful and green.

The Golden Age of the Gods

The prophetess describes this next time period as a golden age. The gods played games, learned new crafts, and peacefully ordered the world. They appointed places for the sun, moon, and stars, and time began to influence the world. The gods then made two humans, a man and a woman, from two pieces of driftwood. The seeress warns Odin that the giants will destroy the gods in the final battle of **Ragnarok**, but then

This illustration of the love goddess Freya appears in a 1915 book called *A Book of Myths*.

tells him that a new world will emerge. Some gods will come back to life and rule a beautiful kingdom in a new golden age. Although the seeress's words are grim, her final prophecy brings hope.

A Beautiful Bride?

"Voluspa" tells a solemn, powerful story, but other stories in the *Poetic Edda* are humorous. Thor, the god of thunder, is involved in many silly adventures. The most charming is "Thrym's Poem." One morning, Thor wakes up and discovers that the frost giant Thrym has stolen his hammer. Thrym will return it only if the gods give him the goddess of love, Freya, in marriage. Instead of sending Freya and putting her in danger, the gods order Thor to dress up as Freya and pretend to be Thrym's bride. Thor is outraged but finally agrees. He puts on a wedding dress and Freya's famous necklace. Loki, the most mischievous god, dresses as a bridesmaid and accompanies Thor to the land of the giants. Thrym, an unusually stupid giant, does not notice that his bride is not Freya, even though Thor does a bad job of acting like a girl.

After Thor arrives at Thrym's mansion, he devours the entire wedding banquet. When Thrym tries to kiss his bride, Thor terrifies him with his bloodshot, angry eyes. Loki soothes Thrym into believing that Freya is merely hungry and tired after her wedding preparations. Finally, Thrym brings out the hammer and lays it in his "bride's" lap. Thor grabs the hammer and clobbers all those who have put him in this humiliating situation.

Skadi and the Shiny Feet

Giants like Thrym will never get along with the gods, but Snorri tells one story in which the gods made peace with an enemy giantess named Skadi. Dressed in armor, she came to fight the gods after the death of her father (the gods had killed him because he fought them for some magic apples). The gods coax Skadi into making peace and suggest that she marry one of them. She wants to marry the beautiful god Balder but, presumably, the feeling is not mutual.

The view of the Norweigan Sea from the coast of Norway is breathtaking. It's no surprise that the god of the sea, Niord, plays a role in Norse mythology, like in the story of "Skadi and the Shiny Feet."

The famous Viking Ragnar Lothbrok wears a red cape and sword in this illustration. Lothbrok is mentioned in a poem by the first-known skáld.

The gods allow Skadi to see only their feet before choosing one of them as her husband. When Skadi sees a pair of shining, white feet, she thinks it must be Balder and chooses him to be her husband. Unfortunately for Skadi, the feet belonged to Niord, the god of the sea. Skadi did not realize that the sea god would have the cleanest, shiniest feet, so the gods were able to offer Skadi a peace pact by marriage without giving her Balder as a husband.

Snorri ends the story by telling us that Skadi and Niord did not get along. Skadi hated hearing seabirds screech, and Niord did not want to live in her mountain homeland, so Skadi spent most of her time there without him. In spite of their bumpy marriage, Skadi remained true to the gods.

The *Poetic Edda* and the *Prose Edda* are full of Norse lore. Some of the myths are powerful and strange. Others are lighthearted. Snorri feared that the stories would be forgotten, but luckily the *eddas* have survived.

Skáldic Poetry

The term "skáld" was first used to describe highly respected court poets of ninth-century Norwegian kings. Many skálds were from Iceland. Their poetry preserved old traditions and was recited by them in courts and assemblies. Skálds told stories of battle, hatred, love, and envy. They also offered praise for kings they wanted to immortalize. Often, a poet's verses were about himself.

Some of the most powerful poetry was based on pictures found on shields. The earliest known skáld, Bragi the Old, authored one such poem. In it, he gives thanks for a shield said to have been sent to him by the Viking Ragnar Lothbrok.

For many skálds, the Norse myths were their main source of imagery. Thus, to refer to a particular deity, skálds often combined a description associated with a particular deity and a god's name. For example, the phrase "Victory Thor" actually referred to Odin.

Skáldic poetry was not easy to understand. It was a highly complex art form that used literary devices such as alliteration, metaphors, and ancient, no-longer-used terms. If a skáld wanted to convey the idea of a "rainbow," for example, he used the phrase "bridge of the gods." For "gold," he would use "the tears of Freya." Eventually written down, skáldic poetry has enabled some historians to reconstruct the early history of the Norsemen.

Opposite: The Karlevi runestone in Sweden includes skáldic verse. It is the oldest recorded skáldic poetry.

The Eddas: Iceland's Lore 29

BAXTERS Patent Oil Printing. 11. Northampton Square.

YGGDRASILL,

3 Yggdrasil, the Sacred Ash Tree

Yggdrasil (IG-drah-sil) stood at the center of the earth, where Odin discovered that its falling twigs formed the runic alphabet. The top of the tree touched the sky, and its roots reached down into the earth. A bright-eyed eagle with a hawk on his beak perched on the topmost branch scanning the four directions. Nidhogg, a huge serpent, coiled around Yggdrasil's base, chewing its three roots. Snakes slithered around the trunk. Squirrel Ratatosk ran up and down the tree between the eagle and the serpent delivering insulting messages. Bees made honey from the sweetness that dripped from Yggdrasil's leaves. Four deer living in the branches nibbled its green shoots. Daily, the three supernatural Norns (these women were known as Past, Present, and Future) mixed sacred water with clay and covered the roots to cure the damage caused by the creatures that attacked the tree.

Opposite: Yggdrasil is also known as the "world tree."

Regions of the Mythological World

According to Norse mythology, the world was divided into various regions: **Asgard**, where Odin, Thor, and the other **Aesir** resided in splendid halls was in the top of the ash tree's branches. Vanaheim was the home of the **Vanir gods**. Alfheim was the home of the light **elves**. And **Valhalla** was where the **Valkyries** and slain warriors lived. The rainbow bridge Bifrost connected Asgard, the World of Gods, to Midgard, the World of Men. Midgard surrounded the land of mortals and kept it separate from Jotunheim, the Land of Giants. In caves below Midgard lived the **dwarfs** and black elves.

Another region was Niflheim, the frozen World of the Dead. At its very lowest depths was Hel, a place of judgment for those who died of accident, disease, and old age. Balancing the cold and frost of Niflheim was Muspellheim, the land of fire.

Supporting Yggdrasil were three mighty roots. Under each lay water. In Asgard, Urdarbrunn was the well where the Aesir met in council. Mimir's well in Midgard was a source of wisdom, and Hvergelmir in Niflheim was a spring that bubbled boiling water. The exact location of

Opposite: Arthur Rackham's illustration of the Norns (Past, Present, and Future)

Yggdrasil, the Sacred Ash Tree 33

each region is unknown, but the sacred ash tree Yggdrasil passed through them all and acted as a life force.

Welcome to Valhalla!

Now, if each race of beings had stayed within the boundaries that are described above and lived peacefully, generations of gods and men might have lived to this very day. But it was in the very nature of the Norse gods to fight and do battle, to seek out new places, and to satisfy their curiosity about the mysteries of the ash tree and its secret treasures.

So it was that the Norse gods were warlike. When fitted with helmets of sturdy metal and swords of shining steel, they battled giants and other gods alike, and many were killed. Humans also fought in Midgard, and many died as a result. But Odin, father of the Norse gods, did not let these fallen heroes—gods, giants, and humans—lie forgotten and unsung. Instead, he built a great, glowing hall, called Valhalla, for them.

The Role of the Valkyries

The Valkyries, Odin's warrior goddesses, swept up the bodies of those who fell and carried them, on their great war horses, to the very doors of the hall. Its roof was

Odin (*right*) hosts a feast. The Valkyries are shown serving food and drinks.

high and lofty, and its walls were lined with weapons of every kind. Eagles soared through its high places, and doves raced along its floors, as if all was part of the world forest itself. The great main doors of Valhalla opened for the fallen gods and heroes, that they might rest and refresh themselves.

Once inside, they were to relax and feast on a mighty roasted boar. Their drink was mead in never-ending streams from the two udders of a magic goat called Heidrun, who fed on the tender leaves of the great ash

Many pieces of art are inspired by the Valkyries, including this painting by William T. Maud called *Valkyries* and Richard Wagner's opera *Flight of the Valkyries*.

tree. Although Valhalla shielded its heroes, and the Valkyries themselves served them food and drink, they all knew that when Ragnarok—the Day of Doom—came, they would leave Valhalla through its hundred doors to do battle with the forces of evil. To this end, every morning, battles broke out inside the hall and continued throughout the day until all were dead. When night descended, they revived, feasted, and drank.

A Protective Web

To help in the final battle that would determine the fate of mankind and gods alike, the Valkyries wove a web of good fortune to ensure victory. The sight of them on the battlefield, brave and fearless astride their immense and fiery steeds, brought a false confidence to Odin and his followers. To tell them when the battle would begin, the god of wisdom, Heimdall, kept a faithful watch on the bridge between Asgard and Midgard. He was looking for any sign of trouble. With his keen sight, he could see approaching armies at great distances, and if he did, he would then raise his Gjallarhorn (a loud horn) to sound the alarm. Heimdall himself would defend the good to the very end, fighting Loki, the trickster god whose evil acts could defeat the Norse gods. And, if that happened, all the heroes would be gone, like Valhalla itself, forever.

4 Balder's Dream

O f all the Norse gods, the kindest, most handsome, and best loved was Balder. Loki, the trickster, who was neither handsome nor kind, was terribly jealous of him. Every time Loki did something that caused Odin displeasure, Balder did something good. He was as easy to trust as Loki was to distrust. After many decades of anger and resentment, Loki needed just the smallest excuse to be rid of him.

Protecting Balder

One night, Balder had a terrifying dream in which he saw his own death. Now all the gods, save Loki, loved Balder, and looked for a way to reassure him. They asked the goddess Frigg to devise a way to protect him. Frigg went to each of the plants, rocks, crags, and thorns and made each promise never to hurt Balder. As Frigg traveled

Opposite: This Viking pendant shows Balder riding a horse.

on, she came to a very small plant, a sprig of mistletoe. "Should I trouble myself with such a young plant?" she asked herself. "Surely it could do no harm to anyone," she thought. "I can return for its oath after it has grown a bit more." So Frigg passed by the mistletoe and, after receiving all the oaths she thought she needed, she returned to Asgard.

Loki had been watching Frigg and felt certain that here was a chance to hurt or even kill Balder. He stopped Frigg and asked, "Were you able to get a promise from every plant?" "Yes," Frigg replied. "And a long journey it was. But they have all sworn oaths never to hurt Balder."

"And you missed nothing?" Loki continued. "Not even the smallest plant, rock, stone, or pebble?"

"Ah, well," Frigg said, "there was one very small plant. I saw no harm in letting it go. I will have it swear its oath when it has grown more."

"Now which plant would that be? You can tell me. Your secret is safe with me."

"Well," said Frigg, who was tired from her long day, "I think it is all right to say it was the mistletoe."

Loki was thrilled. The next day he joined the other gods and suggested that they jest with Balder by tossing

Opposite: Loki would pay a great price for his trickery.

plants and rocks at him to prove his dream false. One by one, the gods raised a rock here, a little leaf or plant there, and threw it at Balder. Everyone laughed as nothing injured him. Then, Loki fashioned a small dart from a branch of mistletoe, placed it in the hands of the blind god Hoder, and, guiding Hoder's arm, threw it at Balder. It hit Balder, and he fell to the ground, dead.

A Plan for Balder's Return

The gods were horrified and heartsick. What could have happened? Did not Frigg herself have every plant and pebble swear not to harm Balder? But she remembered the mistletoe and offered herself to anyone brave enough to ride into Hel and pay for Balder's return.

Hermod, one of Odin's sons, jumped upon Sleipnir, the eight-legged horse, and rode down into Hel. He headed straight through the fogs and mists, the frozen crags and jagged landscape, until he came to Hel herself. (Hel was the daughter of Loki, who ruled over the place called Hel.) He begged for Balder's return to Asgard. Hel told him that if every god, goddess, man, woman, and child would weep for Balder, then he could return to Asgard.

Opposite: Hermod kneels before Hel.

Messengers were sent everywhere, and people and gods alike wept for Balder. But when messengers arrived at the cave of a giantess Thokk, she sneered at them and said, "Why should I weep for Balder, who never did a good thing for me? No, I will not weep for him!" So, Balder's soul was condemned to the frozen depths of Hel.

Shape-shifting Loki

Odin took the god's body and placed it on a funeral pyre on his own ship, *Ringhorn*. Balder's young wife, Nanna, who had died from despair, was also placed on the vessel. A great fire was lit, and the ship was pushed out to sea by a giantess, because Odin was not strong enough to do it alone. Even as *Ringhorn* burned to ashes, it was discovered that the giantess Thokk was none other than Loki in disguise, the single voice that had kept Balder's soul in Hel. This was the final insult to Odin and the other gods. Loki was expelled from Asgard, never to return. No place, however, would be his home for long. As soon as he was found, he had to move, and, in so doing, he changed shapes to remain safe and undetected.

Finally, the gods called upon Honir to fashion a net to catch Loki. When Loki became a salmon in a stream, Honir cast his net and brought him up, straining for air, until he returned to his real form. The gods grabbed him and tied him to three heavy stones. Above Loki, they tied a huge, venomous serpent with its mouth open, dripping poison down onto his head. His wife was allowed to stay beside him and catch the poison in a basin. Each time she took the basin to empty it, the poison dripped into Loki's eyes and mouth, causing him to scream in agony. In his heart, he began plotting the end of the gods.

Ragnarok

With the punishment of Loki and the death of Balder, terrible troubles began on Midgard, the World of Men. The descendants of the ash tree, humans, giants, dwarves, and gods, found themselves in a dreadful series of battles. Ragnarok—the Day of Doom—had come. For three years, war raged in Midgard. Father and son fought each other to the death. Then came the three years of the Fimbul Winter, with cutting winds and biting frosts. The stars fell from the heavens; forests ripped apart. Crags along every coastal plain broke and sank into nothingness. Roaming the earth and destroying every living thing were wild wolves, fathered by the giant wolf Fenrir, the first of Loki's evil offspring. One wolf ate up the moon; another devoured the sun. Then, an enormous earthquake broke

Balder's funeral was a
typical Viking sendoff.

George Wright's illustration
shows of the chaos of Ragnarok,
the Day of Doom.

the magic rope the gods had used to bind Fenrir, setting him loose upon the earth.

A giant tidal wave set free Loki's second child, the hideous and gigantic serpent, Jormungand, whose movements caused more tidal waves, flooding Hel itself. Then, Loki's daughter Hel was unleashed to seek her evil destiny.

Hel steered *Naglfar*, the dreaded Ship of Death, up past the middle of the world tree to Asgard for the final confrontation. *Naglfar* was built from stem to stern with the fingernails of all the dead men since the world began.

Set free from his chains by earthquakes, Loki came with Fenrir, Jormungand, and Hel. First, Fenrir's giant jaws and teeth scraped the skies and dragged along the ground, breaking the sky apart and scorching the earth with flames gushing from his mouth. Next, Jormungand spewed fire and poison, whose fumes enveloped the earth in a disgusting stench.

When the sky split open, out poured a blazing cavalry of fire giants from Muspellheim, the land of fire. They were led by Surt, an evil giant who emerged from his furnace on a fiery horse. It was now that Odin called for his heroes from Valhalla. Heimdall, the watchman,

blew his mighty horn and
out rushed the heroes. The
battle for the end of the earth
was fully engaged. Odin tried
to kill Fenrir with Piercer,
his mighty sword. But as he
raised the blade to strike,
Fenrir leapt up and swallowed
Odin in one gulp. Odin's son
Hermod ripped open Fenrir's
jaws in an attempt to save his
father's life but Odin's limbs,
along with that of the giant
wolf, were strewn across the
land. Thor raised his hammer
over Jormungand's head
and smashed it into pieces
with such force that the
hammer was embedded in the
earth forever.

The Battle Ends
Heimdall had been looking for Loki all this time. It was
his mission to destroy the trickster god. When at last they

Odin faces off with Fenrir during Ragnarok

Fenrir was a fearsome wolf and Loki's oldest child.

met, eye to eye, they raised their swords and, with one mighty thrust, they pierced each other in the heart and both fell dead.

From the south came the sons of Muspellheim, blazing across the sky like a thousand suns. As they rode, all that they passed melted into the sea and soon the universe seemed lost forever. But was it really gone? After the burning clouds had fallen away and there was only darkness, a new sun arose in the sky. Then a new moon appeared as well. The fiery seed of the lost sons of Muspellheim inhabited the new earth.

It is this land where humans now live, some as giants, some as humans, and some as godlike creatures. Whatever became of those little parts of Loki, the trickster, which were tossed into the great unknown? It is said that a bit of him lies in each one of us.

5 Thor's Wedding

The Vikings told stories about gods, giants, and other creatures who lived in other worlds. They told stories about Thor, the god of thunder, and his hammer. His was the only weapon strong enough to fight the evil giants. This is one of those stories.

The Missing Hammer

"You trickster!" Thor shook Loki awake. "Where's my hammer?" Thor's eyes blazed as bright as his fiery beard.

"It's no trick of mine." Loki sprung off the straw mattress as if it were a mound of coals.

"All the gods are in danger without your hammer to protect us from the jealous giants."

Thor and Loki stormed across Asgard, world of the gods, to the goddess Freya's palace.

Opposite: In this painting, Thor, the god of thunder, fights giants with his famous hammer.

"Someone stole my hammer!" Thor's voice pounded the granite walls.

"How will you bless new brides?" Freya's peachy cheeks faded.

"Freya, lend me your feather cloak," said Loki. "I will find Thor's hammer." And he swooped down to Giantland. Thrym, the giant king, lounged on a burial mound.

"Where is Thor's hammer?" Loki flitted around Thrym's boulder-sized head.

"It is hidden." Thrym's lips stretched as thin as the silver moon. "I will return it only when Freya becomes my bride."

That is not so hard, thought Loki. But when he reported Thrym's demand back in Asgard, the goddess of love, Freya, raged.

"Never! That giant's beard is a tangled bramble pile. His eyebrows wriggle like vipers. His thundering feet make my head ache. Never!"

"The council will decide," said Thor.

One week later, the gods gathered at Asgard. "We'll storm Giantland," said one god.

"Without the hammer?" asked another.

"They'll crush us," said a third.

Then Heimdall, the god of wisdom, spoke. "Thor must go in Freya's place. The giants will not recognize him under a bridal veil."

"Never!" Thor cried. "The mighty Thor disguised in lace and ribbons?"

"You will not be so mighty when the giants rule," said Loki. "I will go disguised as your bridesmaid." Loki curtsied. Thor growled.

Thor in Disguise

They dressed Thor in silk and jewels. They masked his beard with a veil. Freya fastened the feather cloak over the bridal costume, and Thor and Loki flew to Giantland.

"She's coming!" Thrym said as he watched the feathered figure descend.

At the wedding banquet, Thor devoured an ox from head to hoof. He swallowed eight salmon and gobbled four trays of cakes. "What an appetite!" said Thrym.

Loki thought fast. "Freya has fasted these eight days out of longing for Thrym and the giants." Loki batted his eyelashes.

Thrym leaned toward Thor's veiled lips. Thor's eyes flashed. Thrym jumped. "What burning eyes!"

Loki giggled. "Freya has not slept these eight days out of longing for Thrym and the giants."

"Bring the hammer to bless the bride," said Thrym. Two giants laid the hammer across Thor's knees. Thor's laughter thundered through the hall. Thrym gasped. "What a deep voice ..."

Then Thor grabbed the hammer and swung it over his head. Thrym's eyes bulged as Thor swung the hammer over and over and over again until Giantland lay silent.

"Hail the lovely Thor!" shouted Loki when they returned to Asgard with the mighty hammer. Thor growled.

Thor's hammer was said to return to him after he threw it, like a boomerang.

Glossary

Aesir The collective name for the main Norse gods and goddesses.

Asgard Home of the Aesir (Norse gods and goddesses).

dwarfs Manlike beings who live in caves and are known for craftsmanship and wisdom.

edda A Norse and Icelandic poetry form.

elves Mythological begins who can be helpful as well as malicious.

giants Principal enemies of the Norse gods.

Ragnarok Destruction of the old world in a terrible battle, accomanpanied by flood and fire.

runes Letters used by Germanic and Norse peoples from about the third century, probably adapted from Greek and Roman sources, and written as magic signs on stone, wood, bone, and metal. Often found on amulets.

Valhalla Hall of those slain in battle; a warrior's paradise.

Valkyries Female beings associated with the god Odin who selected certain of the warriors killed in battle to be transported to Valhalla.

Vanir gods Fertility beings who fought the Aesir and exchanged hostages.

Yggdrasil A sacred ash tree whose branches extend over the whole world.

Further Information

Books

d'Aulaire, Ingri, and Edgar Parin d'Aulaire. *d'Aulaires' Book of Norse Myths*. New York: The New York Review of Books, 2005.

Gaiman, Neil. *Norse Mythology*. New York: W.W. Norton & Company, 2017.

Higgins, Nadia. *Everything Vikings: All the Incredible Facts and Fierce Fun You Can Conquer*. Washington, DC: National Geographic Kids, 2015.

Websites

Write Your Name in Runes

http://www.pbs.org/wgbh/nova/ancient/write-your-name-in-runes.html

Learn more about runes and spell out your own name in this interactive activity from PBS.

Vikings

https://www.dkfindout.com/us/history/vikings/

DK presents a comprehensive look at the Vikings. Take a quiz to test your knowledge, learn about how the Vikings lived, and view diagrams and pictures.

Vikings: Beliefs and Stories

http://www.bbc.co.uk/schools/primaryhistory/vikings/beliefs_and_stories/

Explore photos, videos, and summaries about the Norse and their beliefs.

Page numbers in **boldface** are illustrations.
Entries in **boldface** are glossary terms.

Index